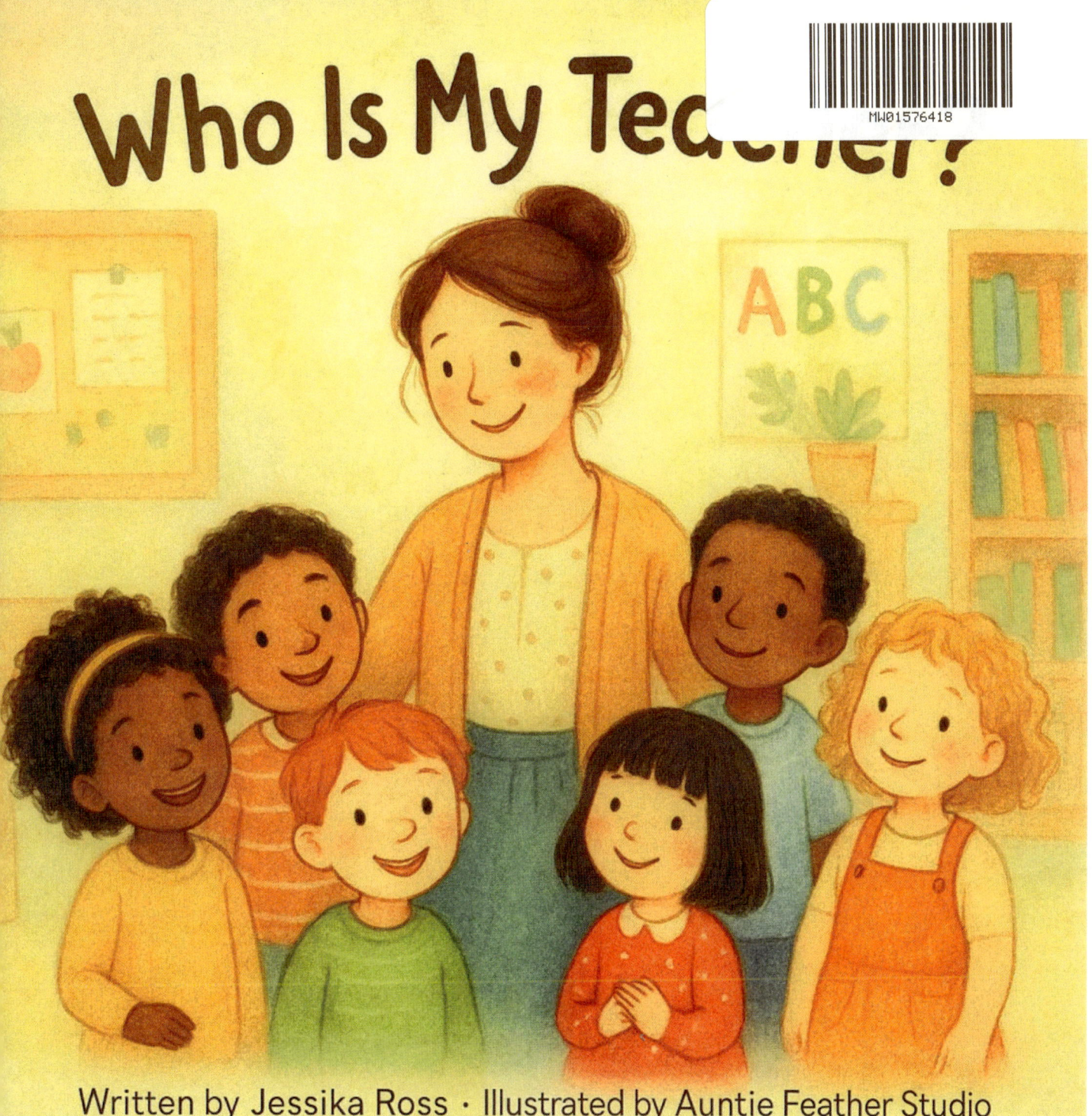

Who is my teacher when school is all done?

Does she stay in the classroom when I'm out having fun?

Does she nap at her desk till the bright morning light,

Or read bedtime stories to her own kids at night?

She might cook spaghetti and laugh as it twirls,

Or paint pretty pictures with her own boys and girls.

Maybe a puppy jumps up with a bark,

Or she takes a slow stroll with her dog in the park.

She might have a garden with blossoms in bloom,

Or sing silly songs while she cleans up her room.

She shops for bananas, and bread, and some rice,

She waits in long lines, just like you—once or twice!

In summer she works at the market or store,

To save up for pencils and notebooks—and more!

Sometimes she's tired, or her car breaks down,

But still she shows up with a smile, not a frown.

She cheers for her child at the big baseball game,

And claps extra loud when they call out his name.

She visits her neighbors and helps them with care,

She bakes little cookies she's happy to share.

But each day she packs up her worries and strife,

To give you her best in your school-day life

So who is my teacher?

A person—it's true!

With hopes and with struggles,
just like me, just like you.

But best of all blessings, she chooses each day,

To guide me with love in her own special way.

Now when I see her, I know from the start,

My teacher is someone with a very big heart.

Made in the USA
Coppell, TX
02 September 2025

53783940R00021